ISLAND HOPPING
IN THE PACIFIC

by

Wallace B. Black
and
Jean F. Blashfield

CRESTWOOD HOUSE
New York

Maxwell Macmillan Canada
Toronto

Maxwell Macmillan International
New York Oxford Singapore Sydney

Library of Congress Cataloging-in-Publication Data

Black, Wallace B.
 Island hopping in the Pacific / by Wallace B. Black and Jean F.
Blashfield. — 1st ed.
   p. cm. — (World War II 50th anniversary series)
Includes index.
 Summary: Explains why it was necessary for allied forces to make their
way through islands up the Pacific on the way to invading and conquering
Japan.
 ISBN 0-89686-567-3
 1. World War, 1939-1945 — Campaigns — Islands of the Pacific — Juvenile
literature. 2. Islands of the Pacific — History, Military — Juvenile literature.
3. World War, 1939-1945 — Campaigns — Pacific Area — Juvenile literature.
4. Pacific Area — History, Military. [1. World War, 1939-1945 — Campaigns —
Islands of the Pacific. 2. Islands of the Pacific — History, Military.] I. Blashfield, Jean F. II. Title. III Series: Black, Wallace B. World War II 50th
anniversary.
D767.B525   1992
940.54'26—dc20

                           92-2505

Created and produced by B & B Publishing, Inc.

Picture Credits
Dave Conant, map - page 15
National Archives - pages 3, 6, 12, 13, 16, 21, 25, 35, 37, 39, 42, 43, 44 (top)
United States Air Force - pages 11, 18, 19, 27, 28 (top)
United States Navy - pages 4, 9, 23, 28 (bottom), 31, 34, 41, 44 (center and bottom), 45 (both)

**CRESTWOOD
HOUSE**
  Macmillan Publishing Company   Maxwell Macmillan Canada, Inc.
  866 Third Avenue   1200 Eglinton Avenue East
  New York, NY 10022   Suite 200
                  Don Mills, Ontario M3C 3N1

Macmillan Publishing Company is part of the Maxwell Communication Group of Companies.

Printed in the United States of America

First Edition

10 9 8 7 6 5 4 3 2 1

CONTENTS

A Japanese dive-bomber plunges downward toward the aircraft carrier USS Hornet while a torpedo plane circles, waiting to strike.

Chapter 1

JAPAN THREATENS AUSTRALIA

On December 7, 1941, World War II had been going on in Europe for more than two years. On that day Japan launched its treacherous attack on Pearl Harbor in Hawaii. That action brought the United States into the war. The United States and its allies immediately declared war on Japan.

Japan attacked and occupied one nation or island territory after another in the Pacific. Many of them were British and Dutch colonies and some were U.S. possessions. Within a matter of weeks the Japanese were far along in their plans to conquer all of Southeast Asia and the islands of the Pacific Ocean.

By June 1942 the Japanese controlled the Pacific Ocean from an eastern line just west of the Hawaiian Islands to the Indian Ocean on the west. They had invaded and conquered almost all of the islands in between, including the Philippines and the Dutch East Indies (now called Indonesia). They also occupied most of Southeast Asia. Their conquests spanned a distance of more than 8,000 miles from east to west.

To the north, the Japanese occupied U.S. territory in the Aleutian Islands of Alaska and controlled all of the coast of China. To the south they had extended the territories conquered to include most of the giant island of New Guinea and the island of Guadalcanal in the Solomon Islands near

Australia. This vast area covered a distance of some 6,000 miles. The victorious Japanese army, navy and air force completely dominated almost all of the entire Pacific region.

The conquest of the Philippine Islands by the Japanese was a bitterly fought campaign. For six months General Douglas MacArthur's heroic American and Filipino armies held out against a superior enemy. Although the Japanese finally won, it was a costly victory and delayed their advance southward. This gave the United States and Australia, its only ally in the South Pacific, more time to prepare for the battles that would soon follow.

Japanese Landings in New Guinea

New Guinea is a large island some 1,500 miles long located just north of Australia. Only 90 miles separate that island and the Australian continent at the closest point. Before capture by the Japanese invaders, Western New Guinea had been controlled by the Dutch. The eastern end, called Papua New Guinea, was still controlled by Australia.

U.S. troops move steadily ashore on New Guinea in the South Pacific in an uncontested landing. Future landings would not be so easy.

Continuing their southward advance, Japanese troops landed at several points on this strategic island in March 1942. During the weeks that followed, more landings were made along the north coast of New Guinea, bringing the Japanese invaders even closer to Australia.

Japanese carrier-based aircraft had already bombed the key northern Australian port of Darwin in February 1942. Following their landings on New Guinea the Japanese established air bases. From there they again bombed Darwin as well as the Australian-controlled city of Port Moresby on the south coast of New Guinea. Finally, after months of retreat, the Allies began to strike back.

U.S. Forces Arrive in the South Pacific

In March 1942, General Douglas MacArthur arrived in Darwin, Australia, where he was appointed Supreme Allied Commander, Southwest Pacific. He had just been evacuated from the Philippine Islands, which were about to fall to the Japanese invading army. Some 25,000 American troops had also just arrived in Australia. They were the beginning of a massive U.S. troop buildup in the South Pacific.

The U.S. and its allies were determined to regain control of the Pacific and eventually attack the main islands of Japan. The U.S. high command developed a strategy of hopping from one island group to another, moving northward to Japan. The first step in implementing this plan was the occupation of the islands of New Caledonia and New Hebrides located to the east of Australia. U.S. troops landed there in early March 1942. These two groups of islands became key supply and training bases for U.S. forces as they prepared to strike back at the Japanese.

During this same period U.S. carrier-based aircraft went into action. Navy fighters and bombers flew across the island of New Guinea to attack the Japanese. They successfully bombed and strafed Japanese ships as they were landing ground forces on New Guinea. The presence of U.S.

flattops (aircraft carriers) in the area caused the Japanese to delay plans for further invasion of New Guinea for several months.

Port Moresby Invasion Plan Intercepted

In April 1942 U.S. naval intelligence officers were successful in intercepting Japanese radio messages and breaking their codes. From information gathered in this fashion it was learned that the Japanese were planning to invade southern New Guinea and occupy Port Moresby. They were also planning to set up seaplane bases on Tulagi in the Solomon Islands to the east.

Three major Japanese forces made up of troopships, battleships and three aircraft carriers were headed into the Coral Sea northeast of Australia to carry out this mission. If the Japanese were successful in capturing Port Moresby they would control all of New Guinea. They would then be in position to station land-based bombers within reach of the entire northern half of the Australian continent. New Guinea and neighboring islands would also serve as ideal bases from which to launch a major invasion of Australia. The Japanese would also be able to intercept and attack convoys bringing supplies from the United States.

To counter this threat, the U.S. flattops *Lexington* and *Yorktown* were ordered to join together and to intercept and attack the invading Japanese forces.

The Battle of the Coral Sea

Japanese carrier aircraft in the Coral Sea first made contact with U.S. naval forces on May 7. The Japanese attacked two U.S. ships, the destroyer *Sims* and an oiler, the *Neosha*. The destroyer was sunk and the *Neosha* severely damaged. No contact had been made with the two U.S. carriers. At the same time, hundreds of miles to the west, a U.S. force of cruisers attacked the Port Moresby invasion force. It was turned back by Japanese air attacks. However,

A U.S. cruiser comes alongside the doomed aircraft carrier USS Lexington, *to assist in fighting fires that are raging out of control.*

the Japanese commanders, fearing further attacks, ordered their troop transports to delay the planned landings.

Seeking the Japanese invasion fleet, planes from the *Lexington* spotted the Japanese light carrier *Shoho.* The lucky navy pilots immediately attacked the enemy flattop and sank it. The overjoyed pilots radioed their carrier, "Scratch one flattop." It was the first Japanese aircraft carrier sunk in World War II and the start of the first major battle between aircraft carriers.

The next morning aircraft from the two opposing flattop forces made contact. Fierce aerial battles took place in the skies over the Coral Sea. Finally each side located the other's carriers. Torpedo and bombing attacks were launched. The Japanese were victorious in that they sank the giant U.S. carrier *Lexington* and forced the U.S. carrier group to withdraw. However, the Japanese carrier *Shoho* had been sunk and the larger fleet carrier *Shokaku* had been seriously damaged. And furthermore, the Port Moresby invasion fleet was forced to cancel its mission and turn back.

The advance of Japanese forces toward Australia had finally been stopped.

Chapter 2

ISLAND HOPPING BEGINS

After fighting off the Japanese invasion force during the Battle of the Coral Sea, U.S. flattops scored a major victory over the Japanese in the Battle of Midway, which took place a few weeks later. In that battle four Japanese aircraft carriers were sunk. A gigantic invasion fleet headed for Midway was forced to retreat. In Washington, D.C., President Franklin D. Roosevelt and his military advisers decided it was time for the United States and its allies to take advantage of their success as quickly as possible. The time had come to start an island-hopping campaign to recapture the Pacific islands that had already been lost to the Japanese.

Guadalcanal Landings

At the time the Japanese had landed on New Guinea they had also taken other key islands just to the east. In the Bismarck Archipelago they occupied two major islands, New Ireland and New Britain. On the eastern tip of New Britain they had established a gigantic army, air force and naval base at the town of Rabaul. In the Solomon Islands just to the north of Australia, the Japanese had set up bases on all but one of eight islands.

General MacArthur wanted to launch an attack directly against the Japanese stronghold at Rabaul but was overruled by the U.S. Joint Chiefs of Staff. Instead, the island of Guadalcanal — with its airfield and its smaller neighbors, Florida and Tulagi Islands, in the Solomons — was the first Japanese-held territory to be invaded.

P-40 Warhawk fighters taxi into position for takeoff at Henderson Field on Guadalcanal.

On August 7, 1942, U.S. Marines under the command of General Alexander "Archie" Vandegrift landed on Guadalcanal and Tulagi. Aided by strong air and naval support they fought a bitter six-month land, sea and air battle with the Japanese defenders.

Fighting from a narrow beachhead just a few miles long and a few miles deep, the marines outfought a superior Japanese force. In the air, brave marine, army and navy pilots flew thousands of missions from the narrow dirt strip airfield on Guadalcanal that was called Henderson Field. Although under continuous bombing from the air and shelling from the Japanese navy, the rugged marines held on to their tiny strip of land and fought back. They finally drove the Japanese from Guadalcanal for good in January 1943.

It was a long and costly battle. There were heavy losses of warships and aircraft on both sides. In addition to battle casualties thousands more suffered from disease. The Americans lost some 6,500 killed and wounded while the Japanese lost more than 25,000 men.

Papua New Guinea Offensive

During the same period Australian and Papuan native troops fought side by side. It was the start of a long and bloody battle for the control of the Australian territory of Papua. Following several unsuccessful landing attempts, the Japanese decided to fight their way through heavy jungle across the Owen Stanley Mountains in New Guinea toward Port Moresby.

The dense jungles made life miserable for both sides. After advancing to within 50 miles of their goal the Japanese were brought to a halt. Australian reinforcements had entered the battle, driving the Japanese back into the mountains.

In September 1942 a U.S. infantry regiment landed at Port Moresby and entered the battle, moving inland. Their

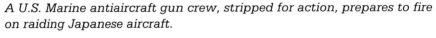

A U.S. Marine antiaircraft gun crew, stripped for action, prepares to fire on raiding Japanese aircraft.

Australian soldiers follow close behind a light tank as they attack Japanese forces in the New Guinea jungle.

mission was to outflank and trap the retreating Japanese. Young and inexperienced U.S. troops fought through the unfamiliar jungles. In October another U.S. regiment was airlifted to a position on the north shore of New Guinea. Now under attack from three sides, the Japanese were slowly being driven back.

Finally, following heavy fighting in some of the most difficult mountainous and jungle terrain in the world, the Allied forces were successful. The Japanese were forced to give up some of their bases on the north shore of New Guinea. By January 1943 the U.S. and Australian forces were on the offensive. Allied casualties in the Papua New Guinea campaign were even heavier than on Guadalcanal. Few battles during the war were fought under the terrible conditions encountered on both New Guinea and Guadalcanal. The fighting in these two campaigns resulted in the first Allied land victories of the war.

The first steps on the long road to Tokyo had been successful.

Chapter 3

RABAUL — JAPANESE FORTRESS

The Allied forces in the Pacific and Asian theaters of war were divided into two commands. The British would be responsible for the fighting in India, Burma and the Indian Ocean, while the U.S. forces would be responsible for the entire Pacific theater of operations. Although the war in the Pacific was basically an American operation, a Pacific War Council made up of all of the Allied nations involved in the Pacific war was formed in Washington, D.C.

General MacArthur's Southwest Pacific Command was responsible for all Allied action in Australia, New Guinea, the Solomon Islands, the Dutch East Indies and the Philippines. U.S. Admiral Chester W. Nimitz was in command of forces and activity in the central and northern zones of the Pacific.

MacArthur Sets Sights on Rabaul

In early 1942 the Japanese had made the town and seaport of Rabaul on the island of New Britain headquarters for all operations in the South Pacific. The Japanese occupation of New Guinea and Guadalcanal and the battles that followed were directed and supplied from this giant base. It was being built into a major command and support facility for Japanese army, navy and air force operations. As a result, Rabaul was a major threat to Australia and the buildup of U.S. forces in the South Pacific.

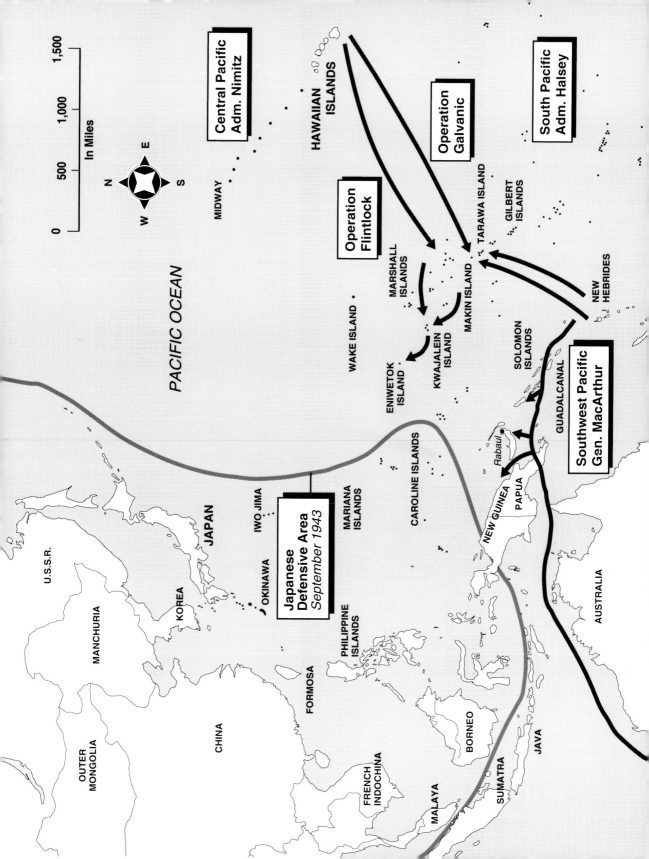

MacArthur's long-range plans called for a return to the Philippines through New Guinea. The Allies would have to fight and defeat the Japanese all along the way. To accomplish this, MacArthur felt that U.S. and Australian forces would first have to capture Rabaul and destroy that base. Placing the South Pacific fleet under MacArthur's command, the Joint Chiefs of Staff in Washington approved his plans.

The first attempt to attack Rabaul was made in February 1942, right after the United States entered the war. A carrier group led by the aircraft carrier *Lexington* had approached within 200 miles of Rabaul. But they were discovered and attacked by Japanese bombers. In the air battle that followed, navy pilot Lt. Edward "Butch" O'Hare shot

Lieutenant Edward H. "Butch" O'Hare seated in the cockpit of his Grumman F4F Wildcat fighter in which he shot down five Japanese planes during a single mission

down five of the enemy planes. He was awarded the Medal of Honor and immediately promoted to Lieutenant Commander. Because the element of surprise was lost, the mission was cancelled and the U.S. carriers withdrew. During the last half of 1942 the Allied forces were completely involved with the battles on Guadalcanal and New Guinea. No further northward advances were possible until these two battles were won.

Operation Cartwheel

It was finally determined that sufficient forces were not available to attack Rabaul in early 1943 as planned. All available forces were needed to continue with attacks northward in the Solomon Islands and in New Guinea. The occupation of Rabaul was postponed until 1944. To prepare for the ultimate attack on Rabaul, Operation Cartwheel was put into action first.

Cartwheel was an ambitious plan to surround and out-flank Rabaul. It called for all of the resources in the South Pacific that the Allied army, navy, air force and marines could bring together. It was to be a two-pronged offensive.

General MacArthur would send his ground forces, with air and naval support, northward along the coast of New Guinea. At the same time, Admiral William F. "Bull" Halsey, Jr., would launch attacks against islands in the northern Solomons to capture and destroy Japanese bases there. U.S. ground troops would conduct amphibious landings in these islands, protected by strong air and navy forces. Together, General MacArthur's and Admiral Halsey's strike forces would form a giant pincer around Rabaul.

Admiral Yamamoto Killed

The Japanese knew they had to stop the U.S. advances in the Solomon Islands to prevent an attack on Rabaul. Admiral Isoroku Yamamoto, commander in chief of the Japanese navy, ordered heavy aerial attacks against U.S.

bases on Guadalcanal. These took place on April 7, 1943. He and other members of his staff planned to make a tour of inspection of Rabaul and neighboring bases on April 18.

U.S. Navy intelligence code breakers intercepted a radio message telling of Yamamoto's flight plans. Top U.S. commanders in Washington planned a secret mission against the unsuspecting Japanese commander.

The 339th Fighter Squadron on Guadalcanal was given the mission of delivering that surprise. Major John Mitchell led a flight of 16 P-38 Lightning fighters equipped with long-range external drop tanks. The planes took off early on the morning of April 18. They were to find and shoot down the aircraft carrying the admiral.

Following a 500-mile flight over water, the P-38 squadron arrived near Rabaul and intercepted Yamamoto's plane,

A P-38 Lightning in flight. Aircraft such as this one, equipped with extra fuel tanks, flew the 1,000-mile mission to intercept and shoot down Japanese Admiral Yamamoto.

A U.S. A-20 Havoc light bomber as it completes a skip-bombing attack on a Japanese freighter

a Betty bomber. It was accompanied by another Betty and six Zero fighters. Outmaneuvering the protecting Zeros, Lieutenants Thomas G. Lanphier and Rex T. Barber attacked and shot down both Japanese Bettys. Yamamoto, a passenger on one of the planes, died in the attack.

Japanese Counterattack

In April the Japanese air force bombed U.S. airfields on Guadalcanal and Tulagi continually. However, superior U.S. Army and U.S. Marine air force units fought off the

Japanese, inflicting heavy losses on the attackers.

Preparing for further Allied attacks in New Guinea, the Japanese sent a large force to reinforce their troops there. In early May a major sea and air battle took place in the Bismarck Sea just north of New Guinea. Four Japanese destroyers and eight transports loaded with 6,000 Japanese troops were sunk. These heavy Japanese losses were a vital blow to their plans for counterattacks in New Guinea. The U.S. Navy suffered heavy losses also, but plans for U.S. island hopping northward in the Solomons continued.

Island of New Georgia Invaded

New Georgia was a key island located about 200 miles north of Guadalcanal in the Solomon Islands chain. It was the next major target in the U.S. offensive northward.

U.S. marine units landed on New Georgia on June 21, 1943. They were supported by landings on other key islands in the New Guinea–Solomon Islands areas. Woodlark, Trobriand and Rendova islands quickly fell and provided additional bases to support the Allied advances. On New Georgia U.S. ground forces, fighting off fierce resistance by the Japanese defenders, advanced steadily.

The Japanese navy supplied its forces in the Solomons with high-speed nighttime missions called the "Tokyo Express." Japanese destroyers escorting supply ships would race down "the Slot" between the northern Solomon Islands. Full-fledged battles between U.S. naval forces and the Tokyo Express took place with heavy losses on both sides. U.S. forces were temporarily stalled in their advances for most of July and August 1943.

However, superior U.S. naval and air forces defeated the Japanese regularly. The Japanese were finally driven off New Georgia. Admiral Halsey's naval and ground forces in the Solomons were now ready to attack Bougainville, the largest island in the Solomon chain.

Dogs were widely used in jungle warfare in the South Pacific. They were trained to search for the enemy, sniff out explosives and carry messages.

Allies Advance on New Guinea

The western prong of Operation Cartwheel was moving forward on the north coast of New Guinea toward Rabaul. The Japanese defenders on the big island were being beaten back steadily.

Beginning in April 1943, Australian and U.S. ground forces began another offensive on the north coast of New Guinea. With skilled support from air and naval forces, the Allies were in full control of key positions in that area by September.

The Allies were now ready to begin the invasion of New Britain toward Rabaul from their strongly held positions on New Guinea. And in the Solomons American marines were occupying one Japanese-held island after another.

Chapter 4

CARTWHEEL ROLLS ON

As the two-pronged attack aimed at Rabaul continued with great success, the Allied high command decided to change Operation Cartwheel's mission. They finally realized that continuing a costly and time-consuming campaign to take Rabaul was unnecessary. The fast-growing U.S. air and naval forces were defeating the Japanese at every turn. The Allies decided to bypass Rabaul since the Japanese forces stationed there were trapped. The Allies could continue on the road to Japan along more direct routes.

New Guinea Campaign Continues

The Japanese were unable to deliver adequate reinforcements and supplies to New Guinea, and so the U.S. and Australian forces advanced steadily. From September 1943 to January 1944 they moved another 150 miles northwest along the New Guinea coast. They had also landed substantial forces on New Britain to keep up the pretense of attacking Rabaul. Although the Japanese defenders were still fighting fiercely in every battle, General MacArthur was moving Allied forces closer to the Philippine Islands.

Every branch of both U.S. and Australian services fought side by side to defeat the Japanese on New Guinea and then on New Britain. It was during this period, with the U.S. Army Air Force in action continually, that Major Richard I. Bong became the highest-scoring ace of all U.S. fighter pilots. An ace was a pilot who shot down five or more enemy planes. Flying P-38 Lightning fighters, Bong downed 40 Japanese aircraft while serving in the South Pacific.

Lieutenant John F. Kennedy, (far right) with his fellow crew members on the torpedo boat PT-109. The future president and his crew performed heroically in sea battle in the Solomon Islands.

Bougainville Island Landings

The next target for the Allied advance in the Solomons was Bougainville Island. A large island, some 150 miles long, it was heavily defended by the Japanese. On November 1, 1943, U.S. Marines, commanded by Guadalcanal hero General Vandegrift, landed on Bougainville. Although they met only slight resistance at first, the marines were in for a long and bitter battle for this strategic island.

During November both sides lost ships in several naval engagements. The Tokyo Express was successful in landing reinforcements on Bougainville. The U.S. forces were confined to a narrow beachhead. On December 9 a U.S. airfield was established on Bougainville and close air support was available. In a few more weeks the Japanese defenders were no longer a serious threat.

After holding the Japanese in check on Bougainville, the U.S. forces continued to surround and neutralize Rabaul. The Admiralty Islands to the west, the Green and Nissan islands to the east, and Emirau Island to the north were all occupied by U.S. forces. Air bases were established on these islands to bomb and harass the defenders at Rabaul while U.S. forces went on to continue Operation Cartwheel elsewhere.

Operation Galvanic

Even while the major battles on the road to Rabaul were being fought, two huge naval forces were being prepared for new attacks elsewhere. As part of an expanded Cartwheel, Operation Galvanic was the invasion of the Gilbert Islands 1,200 miles to the northeast of Rabaul. A task force under the command of Admiral Raymond Ames Spruance sailed from Pearl Harbor in Hawaii on November 10. It attacked Makin Island in the Gilberts on November 20. At the same time, Admiral Halsey sent another invasion fleet from the south to attack Tarawa, a neighboring island in the Gilberts.

Both of these islands had been heavily fortified by the Japanese. Their defenders were under orders to defend their islands to the last man. The American marines suffered heavy casualties, particularly on Tarawa. In the capture of the Gilbert Islands the marine casualties were in excess of 5,000. The Japanese death toll was more than 4,000 — their losses were complete because they did indeed fight to the last man.

Operation Flintlock

With the Gilbert Islands secure, the central Pacific fleet under Admiral Spruance was ready to attack once again. As part of the revised Operation Cartwheel the fleet was headed toward the Philippines from the east.

On February 1 the Flintlock invasion force, also from Pearl Harbor, attacked the Marshall Islands, located some 500 miles north of the Gilberts. The island of Kwajalein, a small coral atoll, was secured in only four days. Again performing heroically and with great speed, the U.S. landing forces overcame another suicidal Japanese defense. More than 8,000 Japanese died while the American marine casualties were less than 2,000.

Just two weeks later Operation Flintlock was extended and the marines attacked the Eniwetok atoll a few hundred

U.S. Marines crawl ashore ahead of an amphibious tank during the attack on Tarawa.

miles to the north. Another fierce battle was fought on this tiny island in the middle of the Pacific. It was also fiercely defended by the Japanese. American marine losses totaled some 1,200, while the Japanese lost their entire force of 3,500 men.

Island hopping had now been extended northward several thousand miles from Australia. The progress of the war in the Pacific was speeding up. General MacArthur was completing the battle for New Guinea that would isolate and bypass Rabaul. He was getting ready to head for the Philippines. Admiral Nimitz, now commander of all U.S. forces in the Pacific, was preparing his massive U.S. naval forces to move farther to the west toward the Philippines.

Chapter 5

THE MARIANAS — GATEWAY TO THE PHILIPPINES

On March 12, 1944, General MacArthur and Admiral Nimitz received new orders. Their next major task was to invade and retake the Philippines and to attack the island of Formosa (now called Taiwan). The target date to achieve these objectives was February 1945.

In the southwest Pacific, the island of New Britain, with the key Japanese base at Rabaul, was completely surrounded and bypassed. The U.S. Army 1st Cavalry Division landed on the Admiralty Islands, northwest of New Britain, as part of General MacArthur's advances toward the Philippines. These islands provided additional airfields for air support for the New Guinea campaign and to further entrap Rabaul.

Leapfrogging up the coast of New Guinea, using amphibious and airborne landings, the Allies captured one Japanese stronghold after another. Finally, on May 27 they landed on Biak Island near the western end of New Guinea. Fighting from well-fortified positions, some 12,000 Japanese troops tried to halt the U.S. advance toward the Philippines.

On June 30 Biak Island fell and one month later the Allies completed the conquest of New Guinea. U.S. forces landed on the Vogelkop Peninsula at the extreme western tip of that war-torn island, effectively ending all Japanese resistance on New Guinea. Those Japanese soldiers who had not been killed or captured were evacuated by sea to find safety on other Japanese islands to the north.

Fifth Air Force B-25 Mitchells dropping "parafrag" bombs on a Japanese airfield. Parachutes delivered bombs right on target as the attacking aircraft flew out of range.

Solomon Islands Battles End

The last major Japanese strongholds in the Solomons were being overrun. Major battles had been fought and won by the American marines. Time and time again the Japanese had counterattacked the U.S. airfields and beachheads. Finally, short of supplies and admitting failure, the Japanese forces began to withdraw. The U.S. forces did not even give chase. The Japanese in the Solomons were no longer considered a threat.

To further weaken the enemy in the south central Pacific, a U.S. carrier force attacked the Japanese naval base on the island of Truk. This giant base, located about 300 miles north of Rabaul, was the major supply and repair base for all Japanese naval operations in the southwest Pacific.

A B-17 Flying Fortress leaves a smoking Japanese target after a successful bombing attack (above). Marine pilots scramble toward their F4U Corsair fighter aircraft (below), *which sit ready for takeoff to intercept and attack Japanese bombers.*

On April 14, 1944, U.S. carrier planes attacked and destroyed that base. Japanese ships in the area fled northward. Truk would not be available to help the enemy during the coming sea and air battles for the Philippines.

Mariana Islands Attacked

With the central and southwest Pacific now under complete control of the Allies, the time had come to make major moves toward the Philippines and the islands of Japan. Major battles against Japanese naval air and sea forces were expected.

Following the loss of six carriers in the Coral Sea, at Midway and in the Solomons, no Japanese carriers had been present to stop the U.S. island hopping in the Gilbert and Marshall islands. However, the Japanese still had a substantial number of flattops that had been kept in Japanese waters close to home. In a last-ditch effort, they were expected to come out to battle the U.S. invasion fleet as it approached the Marianas.

On June 11, 1944, naval aircraft bombed Saipan, the northernmost island in the Marianas, 1,500 miles east of the Philippines. The U.S. task force was the largest group of Allied warships ever assembled in the Pacific. Its mission was to gain control of the Mariana Islands and Guam Island. Control of these islands was vital to the invasion of the Philippines and any attack on the main islands of Japan.

This campaign was being launched only five days after D-Day in Europe when the largest invasion force ever assembled was landing on the coast of France. At last the United States and its allies were able to engage their enemies in force in both Europe and the Pacific.

On Saipan enemy fortifications and air strips were heavily damaged in the pre-invasion raids. On June 15, 1944, two U.S. Marine divisions landed on the beaches of Saipan. Although casualties were expected to be heavy, a U.S. force of some 20,000 marines landed. The Japanese were defending this island outpost with all their strength. An additional large marine landing force arrived two days later and entered the battle. The battle for the Marianas was under way.

Giant Fleets Prepare for Battle

As the invasion of the Marianas took shape, the Japanese gathered their largest naval force since the Battle of Midway. Two separate naval groups had been built around nine aircraft carriers with more than 700 aircraft, five battleships and numerous cruisers and destroyers. They sailed toward the Marianas on June 11 to attack the marines landing on Saipan. However, they were spotted early that day by U.S. submarines and the U.S. fleet was alerted.

To the east, under the command of Admiral Marc A. Mitscher, the U.S. 5th Fleet, a force of 15 flattops and numerous escorting warships, approached Saipan. And following close behind was another huge fleet made up of some six battleships and 20 cruisers. They were ordered to intercept and attack the approaching enemy fleet. The Japanese fleet would be outnumbered and outgunned in every category. The Battle of the Philippine Sea was about to begin.

The Marianas Turkey Shoot

On June 19 Admiral Soemu Toyoda ordered four air strikes launched from his carriers. They were to intercept and attack Admiral Mitscher's force near the island of Guam to the south of the Marianas. Forewarned by U.S. submarine sightings and by early radar sightings, U.S. Navy fighters were airborne and waiting for the attacking fighters and bombers.

Early on the morning of June 19 the first wave of Japanese aircraft attacked. U.S. Navy fighters intercepted and shot down 35 planes in the first wave. No American warships were hit. Following Japanese air strike forces soon appeared on the horizon and navy fighters swarmed into

U.S. Navy Task Force 58 — the greatest naval armada ever assembled — prepares for the Battle of the Philippine Sea near the Mariana Islands.

the sky from all 15 of Admiral Mitscher's carriers.

By the end of the day some 375 Japanese aircraft had been destroyed. Fewer than 30 U.S. planes were shot down. The day's action was the most successful in the war to that date. U.S. Navy pilots were well trained and experienced. The Japanese air force, following heavy losses during the previous year, had only new, young pilots with no combat experience. With superior pilots and aircraft, the U.S. Navy fliers scored a great victory that day, which became known as the Great Marianas Turkey Shoot.

Those few Japanese planes that survived returned to their carriers only to find that two of them, the *Shokaku* and the *Taiho,* had been sunk by two American submarines. On the following day the Japanese fleet was in full retreat. Admiral Mitscher sent his aircraft in hot pursuit and sank the carrier *Hiyo* and several support vessels. The rest of the Japanese fleet withdrew successfully and headed west toward the Philippines and the South China Sea.

With bad weather and the great distances involved in pursuing the enemy, the navy lost some 80 aircraft that were unable to return to their carriers as they ran out of fuel. Further efforts to follow the escaping enemy were cancelled. The Battle of the Philippine Sea had ended in complete victory for the U.S. Navy fliers.

Saipan, Tinian and Guam Fall

After three weeks of bitter fighting, Saipan finally fell to the American marines. The Japanese commanders on the island, Admiral Chuichi Nagumo and General Yoshitsugo Saito, committed suicide. Hundreds of loyal Japanese troops and Japanese civilians followed their example by fighting to the death, jumping off cliffs or committing mass suicide. The Japanese had lost some 27,000 troops while the American losses were more than 16,000 dead and wounded.

On July 21 the American marines landed on the island of Guam, 100 miles south of the Marianas. Saipan's neighboring island, Tinian, was invaded on July 24. By August 10 all Japanese resistance on these islands had ended.

Navy Seabees (naval construction battalions) and the U.S. Army Corps of Engineers went to work on these three islands immediately. Huge air bases and naval facilities were built with two-mile-long runways carved out of the rock and coral of the islands. These islands were intended to be the final stepping-stones for the coming attacks on the Philippines and the main islands of Japan.

Chapter 6

THE PHILIPPINES — MacARTHUR RETURNS

On July 30, 1944, General MacArthur's forces completed the conquest of New Guinea. Over two years earlier he had promised the Philippine people and the world, "I will return." The time to retake the Philippines had arrived. The islands had been in Japanese hands since May 1942.

The U.S. 6th Army and the U.S. Navy 7th Fleet prepared to attack Leyte Island in the southern Philippines. Admiral Halsey's 3rd Fleet approached Luzon, the large main island of the Philippines to the north. The 3rd Fleet would protect the U.S. forces that were to land on Leyte from Japanese naval and air forces coming from the north and west.

On September 15 General MacArthur's forces landed on several islands in the Palau and Moluccas islands on the way to the Philippines. Overcoming stiff resistance from large Japanese army units on these islands, the American invasion forces succeeded in their mission. Japanese air force bases were bombed and destroyed. The enemy ground forces were trapped there until the end of the war. Another barrier to the Philippine invasion had been removed.

Leyte Invasion Force Sets Sail

General MacArthur's orders were to land on Leyte and establish a major base from which attacks on Luzon could be launched. Luzon itself was to be invaded on December

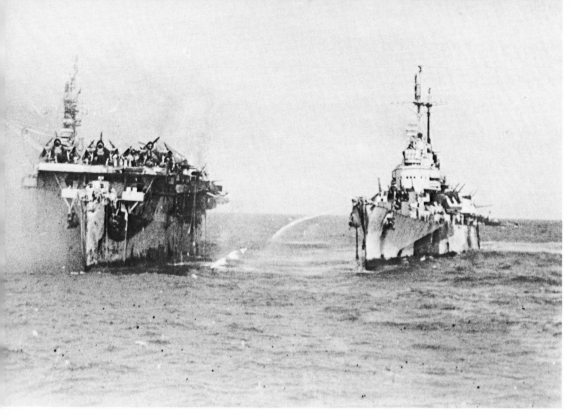

The aircraft carrier, USS Princeton, *ablaze after being struck by a Japanese kamikaze aircraft. Bombed and severely damaged, it had to be sunk by American torpedoes.*

20. On October 12 Admiral Halsey's fleet began major attacks against Luzon and Formosa to draw the Japanese naval and air power away from Leyte.

Admiral Toyoda commanded the combined Japanese fleets in the Philippines and on Formosa. He thought these air attacks were in preparation for U.S. landings on Luzon or Formosa. As a result he ordered all available Japanese air power from Luzon and Formosa to attack the 3rd Fleet. By October 16 the Japanese had lost some 500 aircraft while the U.S. Navy carriers had lost less than 100. While this gigantic aerial battle was going on in the north, General Walter Krueger's 6th Army invasion force set sail from its staging bases in New Guinea.

General Douglas MacArthur (center) *and his staff wade ashore at Leyte in the Philippines, keeping his promise to return.*

MacArthur's Promise Fulfilled

On October 17 American marines successfully landed on islands in the entrance to the Leyte Gulf. Japanese defenses on these islands were quickly done away with, clearing the way for the main invasion force. U.S. forces reached the beaches of Leyte on October 20. The 6th Army stormed ashore along a 20-mile front, meeting only mild resistance from weak Japanese army units. Later that day General MacArthur waded ashore, fulfilling the promise he had made in March 1942 when he was ordered to leave the Philippines. He had returned.

For the next few days the 6th Army continued to expand on the beachhead and soon captured Tacloban, the capital of Leyte, and much of the island. However, the Japanese forces remaining on the island were reinforced and fought back steadily. Heavy rains that lasted for a month further delayed American advances. Fighting the Japanese and the weather, it took the 6th Army all of November before resistance on Leyte ended.

The Battle of Leyte Gulf

Following the successful U.S. landings on Leyte, the Japanese knew that they had to attack and defeat the U.S. 3rd and 7th Fleets. Only if American sea power were destroyed could the Japanese hope to keep hold of the Philippines. What followed was the world's greatest sea battle.

The Japanese high command had gathered together a force totaling some 70 warships. The Japanese navy's 1st and 2nd Striking Forces were ordered to leave their positions in the Dutch East Indies and the South China Sea. They were to attack and destroy the U.S. invasion fleets in the Leyte Gulf and the Philippine Sea to the east of the islands. In an attempt to separate the two U.S. fleets, a force of four Japanese aircraft carriers approached the Philippines from the north. They tried to lure Admiral Halsey's 3rd Fleet away from the Leyte Gulf. With the 3rd Fleet sailing north to meet the Japanese carriers, the American 7th Fleet could then be crushed by the two attacking Japanese Striking Forces.

The plan backfired. When Admiral Halsey learned of the threat of two Japanese fleets of battleships, he turned back to meet them. However, he did send his carriers north to attack the Japanese flattops. On October 25 and 26, in the Battle of Cape Enga, U.S. Navy fighters and bombers attacked and sank Japan's last four flattops.

Facing two complete U.S. fleets in the sea battles in Leyte Gulf and neighboring waters the Japanese Striking Forces were driven back. They lost three battleships and a number of cruisers and other ships. The world's largest battleship, the 70,000-ton *Musashi,* was one of the victims. U.S. losses were heavy and included the aircraft carrier *Princeton* and the escort carriers *Gambier Bay* and *St. Lo.*

Now in full retreat, the Japanese navy was a shambles. The Japanese knew the war was lost. In just three days they had lost all of their remaining carriers and a large number of other warships. The Japanese navy had been

A huge LST (Landing Ship Tank) unloads its cargo in Leyte Gulf as the U.S. forces begin the reconquest of the Philippine Islands.

effectively crippled. It would never again be able to stand up against the superior U.S. Navy. However, during the Battle of Leyte Gulf a new and unexpected Japanese weapon was unleashed. *Kamikaze* (Divine Wind) aircraft made their appearance. Loaded with high explosives and flown by Japanese pilots who were willing to die, these aircraft deliberately crashed into U.S. warships. The escort carrier *St. Lo* was the first of many U.S. ships to be sunk by a kamikaze attack during the closing months of the war.

Landings on Luzon

Because of an extended Leyte campaign American landings on Luzon scheduled for December had been postponed until January 9. On that date the U.S. 7th Fleet delivered a landing force to the Lingayen Gulf, the same place where the Japanese had landed three years earlier. The U.S. had almost complete control of the sea and the air. The landings proceeded rapidly. Even though the Japanese army stationed on Luzon consisted of more than 250,000 men, they were in no shape to fight off the invasion.

Short of food, ammunition and fuel, the Japanese troops retreated before General Krueger's 6th Army. There were fewer than 150 Japanese aircraft left on Luzon and most of these were soon lost in combat. The Japanese continued to resort to kamikaze attacks on the ships of the 7th Fleet. Another U.S. carrier was sunk and two battleships were severely damaged.

The still plentiful U.S. Navy ships continued to bombard Japanese targets in spite of the kamikaze attacks. They cleared the way for more amphibious landings. Soon U.S. forces were pouring ashore on the Bataan Peninsula, the island of Corregidor and south of Manila Bay. Although the Japanese were weakening and being defeated on all fronts, they still continued the fight.

Throughout the months of January and February the 6th Army continued to mop up Japanese resistance in the Philippines. Manila, the capital, was finally captured on March 3 at great cost in Japanese, American and Filipino lives. The main fighting on Luzon had ended. Japanese forces on the other islands in the Philippines continued fighting until the end of the war.

The island hopping from the Solomon Islands to the Philippines had been successful. The large island of Formosa was still targeted for attack. The islands of Iwo Jima and Okinawa also stood in the path of the advancing U.S. forces as they moved toward Japan.

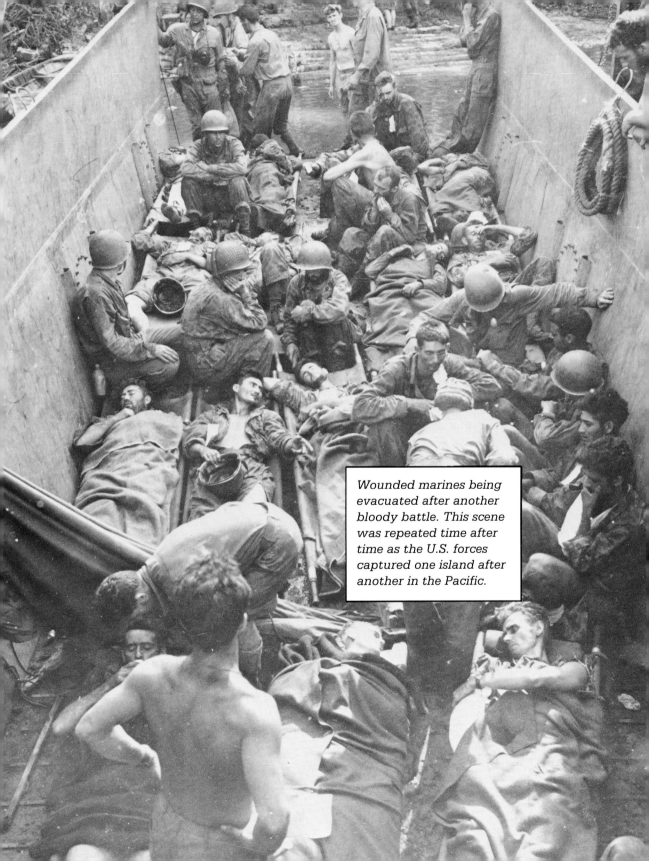

Wounded marines being evacuated after another bloody battle. This scene was repeated time after time as the U.S. forces captured one island after another in the Pacific.

Chapter 7

NEXT STOP — IWO JIMA

As the battles for the Philippines got under way, U.S. commanders could not agree where to attack next. Admiral Nimitz wanted to attack the island of Formosa and the southern coast of mainland China near Hong Kong. This plan was not feasible because supply lines to support such an attack would be too long. Furthermore, U.S. air force bases in China that would have supported such attacks had been knocked out by the Japanese.

General MacArthur thought that if landings on Luzon were successful, Formosa could be bypassed and the main islands of Japan attacked next. As Luzon fell, plans and preparations for a final assault on Japan got under way.

B-29s Arrive in the Pacific

In October 1944 B-29 Superfortresses began operating from the islands of Saipan and Tinian in the Marianas. The giant aircraft could carry sufficient fuel and bombs to attack Japan. Airfields in the Marianas had been built to accommodate B-29s of the 21st Bomber Command. Additional B-29s of the 20th Bomber Command stationed in India and China joined the earlier arrivals during November. They were ready to start bombing the main islands of Japan.

The first B-29 raids on Japan were made on November 24, when aircraft from the Marianas bombed war factories near Tokyo. Although little damage was done in these early raids, the morale of the Japanese people dropped to a new low. Bombing from high altitudes without fighter protection was difficult. Losses of B-29s to Japanese fighters began to rise as the aerial defenses of Japan were strengthened. The only answer was to capture the island of Iwo Jima, which was only 600 miles from Tokyo. Long-range American P-51 Mustangs could be stationed there and provide fighter protection as the big planes flew in to bomb Japanese targets from lower altitudes.

LeMay Commands 21st Bomber Command

In January 1945 General Curtis LeMay took over command of the 21st Bomber Command. His first job was to soften up Japan as U.S. forces landed on Okinawa. General LeMay, a tough, cigar-smoking individual, had achieved great success in directing B-17s bombing Germany. He brought his combat experience and ability as a leader to the Pacific.

On March 9 he ordered a massive night raid by some 300 B-29s. Their target was Tokyo and the giant planes were

A B-29 Superfortress comes in for a landing on one of the airfields in the Marianas. It was from these airfields that attacks against the islands of Japan were launched.

filled with incendiary bombs. Protected from Japanese fighters by the darkness, the B-29s unloaded their bombs on the heart of Tokyo with deadly accuracy. More than 16 square miles of the city, which included many aircraft factories and other war industries, was destroyed by fire that night. Additional incendiary-bomb attacks were made on other targets during the following weeks. The war that the Japanese people had backed for so many years had finally come to their homeland. They began to taste the horrors of war firsthand.

U.S. Marines Land on Iwo Jima and Okinawa

On February 19, 1945, two divisions of U.S. Marines landed on the heavily fortified island of Iwo Jima. Bitter fighting on both sides went on for weeks. The casualties were tremendous. Acts of great bravery and personal sacrifice were abundant among defenders and invaders alike.

Armored landing craft, loaded with U.S. Marines, surge through rough seas toward Iwo Jima.

Mount Suribachi, clouded with the smoke of battle, lies in the background as U.S. forces storm the beaches of Iwo Jima.

The Japanese knew that if Iwo Jima was lost their homeland would suffer even greater damage. The American marines knew that capturing Iwo Jima would provide badly needed fighter bases to protect the B-29s raiding Japan. Iwo Jima was declared secured on March 14. Ten days later U.S. forces launched Operation Iceberg, the invasion of the island of Okinawa, located in the Ryukyu Islands 300 miles south of Japan.

The battle for Okinawa ended on June 22. The island-hopping campaign was over. Finally, the Allies began to prepare for a campaign that never happened — the invasion of Japan itself. The dropping of atomic bombs on Hiroshima and Nagasaki on August 6 and August 9 forced the Japanese to surrender, ending the war.

A Closer Look at . . .

General Douglas MacArthur (left) – *Commander in Chief Allied Forces in the South-West Pacific, General MacArthur led the Allied forces northward in the campaign to recapture the Philippine Islands. One historian stated that MacArthur's "strong personality, strategic grasp, tactical skill, operative ability and vision put him in a class above Allied commanders in any theater."*

Admiral Chester W. Nimitz (right) – *He was commander in chief of the American Pacific Fleet throughout the war. From the victory at the Battle of Midway until the complete defeat of the Japanese navy in the Battle of the Philippine Sea, Admiral Nimitz provided superb leadership at all times. Together with General MacArthur he masterminded the island-hopping campaign across the Pacific.*

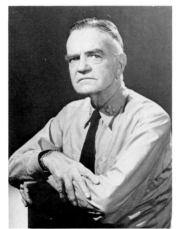

Vice Admiral William E. "Bull" Halsey, Jr. (left) – *A brilliant and skilled naval air commander, Admiral Halsey played a key role throughout the entire Pacific campaign. From the launching of the Doolittle Raid on Japan from the aircraft carrier Hornet to the final aerial battles supporting the invasions of Iwo Jima and Okinawa, he was a superb leader.*

A Closer Look at . . .

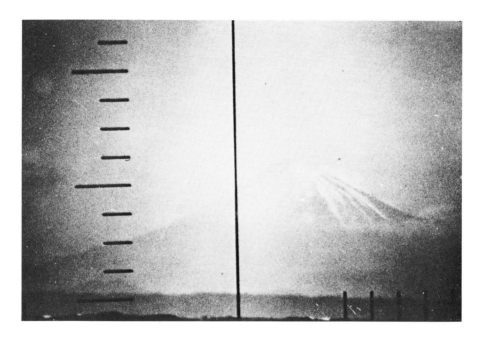

Mount Fuji (above), *60 miles from Tokyo, Japan, as seen through the periscope of a U.S. Navy submarine*

An American submarine (below), *cruising on the surface off the coast of Japan. The silent service, as the submarine service of the U.S. Navy is called, provided constant support in the Pacific, sinking hundreds of Japanese freighters, transports and warships. Fifty-five American submarines and their heroic crews were lost in action in the Pacific theater.*

GLOSSARY

ace A pilot who has successfully destroyed five or more enemy aircraft.

aircraft carrier A flat-topped ship on which aircraft take off and land.

airlift Delivering troops and supplies to a destination in a speedy manner or when surface transport is blocked.

Allies The nations that opposed Germany, Italy and Japan during World War II: Great Britain, the United States, the Soviet Union (Russia) and France.

atoll A circular reef formation and island with an enclosed lagoon.

atomic bomb Any bomb deriving its power from the release of nuclear energy such as those dropped on Hiroshima and Nagasaki in Japan.

battleship The largest modern warship.

beachhead A position on an enemy shoreline captured by invading troops.

cruiser A high-speed warship, next in size to a battleship.

destroyer A small naval vessel used to accompany other ships.

kamikaze Japanese for "divine wind." During World War II the aircraft that were loaded with explosives and the pilots who flew them on suicide missions by crashing the aircraft into enemy ships.

submarine A naval vessel that can operate on the surface or underwater and is armed with deck guns and torpedoes.

troop transports Large merchant vessels equipped to carry troops and their equipment into combat areas.

INDEX